Sort It!

Dona Herweck Rice

We can **sort** anything! You name it, we can sort it.

3

4

3

2

4

6

Sort it by look.

big

round

Sort it by smell.

sweet

stinky

Sort it by taste.

Sort it by touch.

Sort it by sound.

quiet

loud

Think about how things are like other things.

cute

moms
and
babies

Think about how things are *not* like other things.

speed

Then, name them. We name things to **classify** them.

flowers

vegetables

trees

animals

That is how scientists sort things. We can sort things, too!

Let's Do Science!

How can you sort things?
Try this!

What to Get

- classroom items, such as an eraser and a paper clip
- paper and pencil
- tub of water

What to Do

1 Make a chart like this one.

Item	Float	Sink
coin		
eraser		
paper clip		

2 Place each item in the water.

3 Write an X in the chart to show if each item floats or sinks.

Glossary

classify—put things that are the same in groups

sort—put in groups

Index

Your Turn!

Close your eyes. Have a grown-up put things in front of you. Use your senses to guess what they are.

Consultants

Sally Creel, Ed.D.
Curriculum Consultant

Leann Iacuone, M.A.T., NBCT, ATC
Riverside Unified School District

Jill Tobin
California Teacher of the Year
Semi-Finalist
Burbank Unified School District

Publishing Credits

Conni Medina, M.A.Ed., *Managing Editor*
Lee Aucoin, *Creative Director*
Diana Kenney, M.A.Ed., NBCT, *Senior Editor*
Lynette Tanner, *Editor*
Lexa Hoang, *Designer*
Hillary Dunlap, *Photo Editor*
Rachelle Cracchiolo, M.S.Ed., *Publisher*

Image Credits: p.24 Image Source/Alamy; p.7 Nataliia Prokofyeva/Dreamstime; p.17 (top) Agnieszka Kirinicjanow/Getty Images; p.17 (bottom) Rick Gomez/Getty Images; p.16 (right) iStock; pp.18–19 (illustrations) J.J. Rudisill; all other images from Shutterstock.

Library of Congress Cataloging-in-Publication Data

Rice, Dona, author.
Sort it! / Dona Herweck Rice.
pages cm
Summary: "It is time to learn what scientists do."—Provided by publisher.
Audience: K to grade 3.
Includes index.
ISBN 978-1-4807-4535-3 (pbk.) —
ISBN 978-1-4807-5144-6 (ebook)
1. Science—Methodology—Juvenile literature.
2. Readers (Primary) I. Title.
Q175.2.R53 2015
507—dc23

2014008939

Teacher Created Materials
5301 Oceanus Drive
Huntington Beach, CA 92649-1030
http://www.tcmpub.com

ISBN 978-1-4807-4535-3

Printed by: 51497
Printed in: Taiwan